GW00673817

Ysella Mae's Poems by My Father
The Companion Book to "Reciprocity" by Ann Charles

Ed: Chris McQuillen-Wright

First Published Great Britain 2020 by Kerdh Ltd

ISBN 9780955965043

Cover Photograph by Scarlett Gregory

Printed and Bound in Great Britain by Kingdom Print CIC,
Helston, Cornwall

Introducing the Collection

The character of Ysella Mae's father is an enigma in the story. There is a lot of description and a lot of theology, but the character himself is dead before the story begins. Hence the book feels in some ways of exploration of bereavement which indeed it is. Bereavement in all its stages, including seeing elements of loved ones in others; be that mannerisms or stories, memories or language.

These poems are a collection of a simple Parish Priest on his spiritual journey. Some will resonate, some will not. All were written from a longing to gain a deeper understanding of the relationship between God and humanity or is humanity and God?

Foreword

by +Philip Mounstephen, Bishop of Truro

"The stained glass windows in our old churches tell stories in words and pictures as the light shines through them. In many ways that's just what these poems do as simple but profound words create compelling images in our own mind's eye - and touch our hearts and souls. That's what I found as I read. I hope that's what you find too."

Reciprocity

You have left me but what can I say.
Was it just yesterday feels like forever and a day.
But you are with me as you always were
In the clear days, and those lost in a blur.

You are the coaster on the breakfast table
Left forever for I am yet unable
To put it away hidden in the draw
For you always had your coffee there, that I cannot ignore.

You are the coat hanging from the hook,
Yours is the bedside table with its book
Still half read, do you now know the end?
I leave it there, just in case, just to pretend.

I know you're gone, it has to be
Its just a moments each day I will see
You in the small things of everyday
Then I know you're with me, in every way.

Poem for the Ascension
Brother Francis/Brother John

The Feeling that wells up inside
Is something I feel occasionally.
I wish I could control and hide
It, but it takes me over so subtlety
I do not really, fully understand
What makes my heart increase,
The sweat glistening on the palm of hands.
I do know that it brings a kind of peace,
A warmth of heart, a still of the soul.
As I look and raise my eyes heavenward
My hands lifted in silent extol.
Maybe it is brother sun or sister moon,
God's creation giving life to you and me.
One day we'll find the answer too soon,
Our role in praise of the creator we'll see.

Solitude

Tell me what you see
And I'll tell you that is, what is
Tell me you have the key
And I'll let you in; hers and his.

You'll tell me you understand
But I'm not sure you have taken the care?
To some maybe life is so planned
But if that be so why do we care?

Just take me rather to the place
Where I can dream of what may be
Not needing to chameleon my face
Instead I can be straight forward me.

No pretence of the psychiatrist's chair
No false air of solemnity
But rather me on show if you dare
Look, don't touch and never pity.

For my heart is known to me alone
Occasionally it transmits to another
But don't let that affect your tone
Treat me as your sister, brother.

Look at me, that is all I ask
Take me for who I am
It requires no big effort this minor task
Just let me be, who I am.

Worship is Poetry

Worship is poetry. Living is prose.
Worship is the only time
We have the opportunity
To partake in poetry
To come away from life,
Lose ourselves.

Can we really Speak to God
Through Poetry or Prose?
Surely our prayers
Are just ramblings, our poetry
False to a higher truth
Our prose U numbing.

Our tools of our faith,
The religiousity, the Bible,
The liturgy, the ethics, the hymns
And the structures are all there
To bring us nearer to God.
Not to be like the divine,
Not to judge.

But in full humility to move closer beyond
what we think of. Metaphors,
explanations, allegory,
signs and symbols,
in short poetry not prose,
imagination not reality brings us closer to God.

Pentecost

Moving through me but not of me
Seeing within me
The true light not seen
Telling, guiding, imploring what could be
My response is to look elsewhere from me I flee.

Words spoken loudly, deafening my mind
Voices clamouring a sign
Eyes not seeing the wind
Searching, looking, that is not blind.
Take a step and hear the you there , you'll find

There from the beginning
Not always understanding
The divine of loving
To comfort, support always indwelling
There to grasp right now whether known or believing.

Not just to the faithful
To all is the call
Pre-existent before our fall
Part of what is, has been, and forever shall
Be, the part of you and me and whatever shall be-fall.

The Trinity

It isn't about you, it isn't about me
It is about us the new identity.
I am still me and you are are still you
It is just there's something special now
A new unity.

To see in the face of another all that is true
We must recognise in each other ourselves too.
Many faces of a singular person
Many relationships in many situations
Creation continues.

There is something about not knowing
Or totally grasping
An idea, a concept,
Sometimes all there is, is a leap without safety net.
Believing nurtures..

The relationship between us
Me, you, plus one, plus plus
Determines something special
Gives expression to that to be known.
Community lives.

Do not try and recognise
Or make logic from signs
The heart is the strongest
And yet feelings unseen
Love is real.

The Moment

This is the moment that begins the rest of your lives.
You can worry, be anxious and be concerned
about where the future will take you.
But then you won't truly live,
you wont appreciate each other and the love you have.
If you spend your lives expecting,
you will either be disappointed
because it hasn't happened
or you will feel self fulfilled that your prophecy is reality
and you will tell the world, who won't be listening, I told you so.
For the world becomes deaf to the anxious
for we are all full of own worries
and can't absorb everybody else's.
Instead stop, take time to look at the view,
smell the daffodils listen to the birds
and absorb the poetry of life.
Live in this moment,
it is the same moment of eternity
for tomorrow never comes.
This is today and always will be.
So as you begin this new moment,
this today will transform your tomorrow always-
Carpe Diem
seize the day.

A Prayer to Love

It is not that I want to say hello
For I am glad for you, that we have said goodbye.
It's just that I miss you, I could almost choke.
When the tears subside, I smile with a little sigh
Because after all why should I cry
When every goodbye
Is just that little pause before the next hello?

Give me the grace to let you go,
Give me strength to hold you close,
Give me patience for that which I don't know.
Give me hope that all our joy
Will be treasured forevermore
My heart will never be poor
For having known you.

For all the love we shared
The smiles exchanged together.
For all the times you cared
Making my life float as a feather.
You will always be remembered
Grafted in my life, treasured
Adored and with us evermore.
Amen

A Real Prayer

O Lord, my heart trusts in thee
But I do not trust myself.

My mind searches for thee
But gets confused in its machinations.

My soul yearns for thee
But does not know where to find thee.

My life is dedicated to thee
But Does not truly understand dedication.

And so in my relationship with you
I ask you to take control because I lack,

I ask for your help because I am scared.
I have got it wrong so often now its your turn.

For my sake not for yours I ask for help,
For into your hands O' Lord I commend my Spirit.

Mirror
(John Miller Figure in Mauve Interior)

If this was a mirror
How would I feel?
Am I alone or independent?
Am I in isolation or unique?
Do I need someone
Or have I stepped away?
If this was a mirror
What do I see?

If this was a mirror
Would I move away
To find someone or I am content?
What does my heart say?
Where are my emotions?

Do I want someone to come?
If this was a mirror
Who do I see?

Nature knows when the lonely die

The trees above
Cry our tears tears.
They feel the love
Of many years.

The earth below
Receives; it's loved.
The love now sowed
Peaceful as a dove.

The beach nearby
Cries in distress
The butterfly
Brings tenderness.

The river flowing by
Will never end
Hear the goodbyes
As you reach heaven.

Distant Land

On the shore today I stand;
My eyes drift out to sea,
The ships I've known so well in port;
now take their leave of me.

The open sea before them lies
All treasures, in their hold
The happiness they've shared with me,
And the stories they once told.

As they sail further out to sea;
My memory holds them dear
and though each wave takes them away,
my mind's eye sees them clear.

Empty stands the far horizon,
And though I can see you not,
Somewhere in a distant land
They welcome you to port

Through faith I know they have arrived;
With all the gifts they bare,
And though they gave a lot to me,
They have yet more to share..

Dying is but the truth my friend,
as hard as now it seems,
And though you've gone from where you were.
I hold you in my dreams.

Glyn Valley

It is not that I want to see you wave hello
for I am here having just said goodbye.
Its just that I wouldn't mind a little wave
from the green lawn expanding in front of me.
A little wave to say, "Hi! I'm alright now."
Maybe you could wave and turn and walk
down to the woods at the bottom of the field
and slowly disappear, but then I miss you
so would I feel any better at all?

I know you're like one of those lambs
playing frantically in the field.
I know you're as happy as you ever were,
having found a peace I can only dream of.
I know you're loved by the great eternal Shepherd.
A love I cannot imagine. But with the small love I have
I raise my eyes heavenward maybe just maybe
to catch a glimpse of you amongst the clouds.
I know it won't happen.

Instead you've gone through the gate,
like a lamb responding to the call of the shepherd.
Through the gate you've gone to a far
and distant place just over the hill. And I know
that one day I will tread that same journey
and go through that gate to join you.
For it is that gate that I am drawn to,
no matter which path I take through the field of life.
Until I reach it, I will always hold you.

The Flower of the Soul

The flower of the soul lay covered in creation.
The earth nourishing and encouraging the
Little seed of life. The shell was broken
And the very first signs of tentative vulnerability
Shoot upward to the sky. The danger of the birds
Is ever present but somehow this little
Seed seems protected. The shoot reaches further
To the son and slowly but surely the shoot
Becomes a stem. Stronger now rooted in
Creation it begins to branch out. Tiny branches at first
Each growing bigger and stronger. It is watered and fed

Full of promise of a new age of beauty.
And then one day the first realisation of a
Beautiful life. The flower in full bloom, blossoms
Opening always heavenward, feeding the bees with
Its honeyed soul. A soul gasping for more
Sun, spreading itself open, more vulnerable, more beautiful.
Within the protective petals a little seed caught by
The prevailing wind is carried to begin again.
And the flower in the midst of life is taken from us,
Some say to bring happiness and beauty to others.
That may be, but for me that flower always had
Its place right here with me. And I shall
Miss it so, what we shared that little flower and me.

Infinity

If I understood what I was looking at
If I understood why it affected me
I would understand little of that in front
And more of what is within me.

If I understood that my eyes could see
Only what the light lets in
Then I would understand not to look optically
But see with the essence hidden within.

I will understand to see more clearly
And I cannot look with my eyes.
I will understand, I will see with my heart
And understand the infinity that stretches beyond.

I understand that what my heart sees in front
Is only as far as deep within.
I understand myself and as I look
And see more clearly who and where I am.

Living

Life is for living
Each single moment
Sharing together
All that we have.
Let us remember
We are together
Loving and giving
This life we share.

We are so special
Each individual
Let us remember
Each other in prayer.
Rejoicing and crying
Each individual
Is treasured and lovéd
Now and always.

The sun sets this evening
Descending to darkness.
We tremble and fearing
"Where is the light?"
Tomorrow it rises
Lighting our moments
Rejoicing together
We always live on.

Life is eternal,
For everlasting.
The journey is onward
Never the end.
Death is defeated
We will remember,
All whom we love now
Till 'morrow we meet.

Music on a Summer's Night

The rhythm moves me
It takes me places
I've never seen
Uplifting to another land
So far away, amazing,
Totally unplanned.
The notes, basses and trebles
Leading to melody and swing
All meeting, complete in harmony.
It is within this harmony
That we find the truth
That we are all to see.

Our being is meant to be
In balance, no noise,
No silence; one equal music
Taking us further into ourselves
Enquiring and seeking
Opening doors, like discovering shells
Of different sorts on a forgotten
Sea shore. For the truth
That is within was begotten
From the beginning, it is this
We seek through each door
With music as our eternal key.

Seeing is Believing

This day, This day
Seeing is believing
Doing is understanding
Guiding is learning

This day, This day
Yellow is purple
Land is sky
Eyes are soul.

This day, This day
Darkness is opening
Fading is brilliant
Less is more

This day , This day
Is unique
Never tomorrow
Yesterday is gone

This day, This day
We're left with this day
Just this day
Today.

Him

He stares into space, as you pass him by,
As you pass him by, he sits, huddled,
Huddled he sits, his eyes fixed on- nothing.
His eyes, fixed on nothing, not fixed on reality,
Reality is unfixed,
He has escaped from reality.
Escaped from reality; it's too painful to face.

Facing the pain of hunger, thirst, rejection, confinement,
Hungry, thirsty, rejected, confined.

What is the point of living? Living has a point?
What hope is there?
Hope, where?
When reality passes him by, passing him by the reality
Of shoppers laughing.
The laughing shoppers
Do not notice the huddled figure; the huddled figure notices them,
He sees their faces, their faces see his
Embarrassed now, they continue; they continue, their
embarrassment does not.

He disappears from memory; their memory lets him disappear,
He is nothing to you,
You are nothing to him

The Spiritual Promptings

I wouldn't listen, I didn't want to know,
How could I actually dare say I wanted to go
The writings of messages in so many ways
Of friends, of enemies, of busy and lazy days.
So many promptings of the heart
So many questions I didn't know we're to start.
Until I let it go.
I'd held onto long, stamping, No!
Shocking to all, even to me!
But now through the fog I could see
Something's left unfinished are still stilled,
Time to move on, time to be filled.
God has spoken, has done for so long
But now I've listened and simply replied, "Thy will be done."

A Poem on Despair

I walk alone through the streets,
No one cares, no one speaks.
The pavement for my bed,
No pillow for my head.
I sit and I watch,
People giving not much.
O' how can I live
When I have fallen through the sieve.
I am told rest assured
The kingdom isn't far
Blessed are the poor
As they close the front door.

I walk alone through the streets,
Legs a' bare, stilettos for bed
I lie in the bed
Wishing I were dead.
He finishes at last,
I'm suddenly in the past.
He pays the money
To the girl he calls his bunny
I am told to give it up,
But where is the cup?
I need to live,
But no one else will give.

I walk alone through the streets,
I don't see, only weep.
Needing a fix
No longer for my kicks.

Cont.

It's done too much harm
Injecting in my arm.
I am floating in the sky
It's easy to fly.
But then I return
You show your concern
But cannot forgive,
Then how can I live?

I walk alone through the streets,
Not really, I only cheat.
Lying in bed,
Not long till I'm dead.
They say I'm to blame
As I live in pain.
I was in love,
Soon to be a dove.
I've turned another page
Remaining in this cage.
You say you care,
At home in your chair.

Compline

The evening draws nigh my friends,
The sun has set, the sky descends
To let us know it is near the end.
It is dark and whimsical
Hiding its many secrets increasing
As time nears the fall.

The night air beckons, welcoming
Chastening, all encompassing
Taking our joys and swallowing
Them into tomorrow
For the measure of the night
Is found in the talk of the morning.

And if it is forgotten, out of sight
Then the moon and the stars are morning.
For the forgotten hours that we have
Are precious at the end.
So take heed my friends
Take this night into the morrow.

For each night has at its end
The joy of the rising dawn.
New awakenings are only found
From within the experiences
Of sight, soul and sound.
This night is precious now, let the moment last.

Take then, this night
To the morrow, treasure it all
Every moment with all your might.
May it bring the piece you need
To lighten your load with sleep
From the yoke of burden may you be freed.

Flowing Water

Let's find away
Today,
That can take us to tomorrow.
Follow that way
A way like flowing water

Let's leave behind
The things that do not matter,
And turn our lives
To a more important chapter.

Let's take the time
Let's try to find
What real life has to offer
And maybe then
We'll find again
What we have long forgotten
Like a friend, 'til the end,
It will help us onward.

The Sun is high
The road is wide
And it starts where we are standing
No one knows
How far it goes
For the road is never ending.

It goes away
Beyond what we have thought of,
It flows away,
Away like flowing water.

The Call

Come and get me if you dare
I'm too bad for those who care,
They talk of calling but I don't know
Where I reap its cos others sow.
I'm disdained by those holy Joes,
I'm despised, rejected a man of sorrow.
A glorious King they proclaim each night
Well when I see him I'll give him affright.
He wouldn't survive real life with me
Cos I've got it all, shady deals, murder, all to see.
He's reject me this King above
But.......what do I see, a simple dove?
What me, me too, loved so dear ?
A love that knows no boundaries, translucent clear.
A love that forgives everything time and again,
A love intoxicating, encapsulating, nothing is a problem
A love that will conquer all fears within,
A love that doesn't recognise or judge my sin.
A love that is free without commission,
Love that will spread through the world "his" mission.
Forget the religion and all it's trappings,
Its rules, its clothes, hymns and ponderous singing.
Forget the people all holy and wise;
Forget it all? Now that's a surprise.
Start from the beginning a genesis moment
And finish with a revelatory prophetical lament.
Love is at the beginning and the end, in between
Alpha and Omega for love is not seen,
Not analysed or scrutinised or radicalised at all

Cont.

For love stretches back beyond the fall
Of humanity from it's pedestal with God on high
A love that releases what shackles that I may fly .
Why me? You ask, What good did I do?
Secretly help old ladies or visit those sick with flu?
No none of the above, I was as bad as bad
It's such a shame this love came later, but, no time to be sad.
We are loved for who we are, no questions, no tests or
commandment or ten
Simply are loved, you and me. Amen, Amen. Amen.

ColouraBILITY

Colourability
Vulnerability
On the line
Effably sublime.
Total light
In your sight
No darkness
Light in starkness.
Cannot hide
Your vulnerable side.
If Colour is you
How much is blue?

The Unattended Moment

See it whilst standing
Acknowledging, submerging let go of all that is within.
Watching the torrents become ever smoother
Slowly vanishing out of sight, the ebb and flow of flowing water.

See within whilst sitting
Wrestling, arguing with the true self, letting the self win
Against all the buffeting of the world
Slowly becoming stronger and letting it go like flowing water.

See without whilst praying
Silencing the still small voice of betrayal, hurt, letting it go
Into a flood of past and future worries
Letting yourself be purified and washed with flowing water.

Remembrance

To watch the sunset low in the Western Sky
To see the dust settle from the day of war
The only way to look and live, to survive
Is to stare not a head but at sky or floor.

To look for hope when all is despair
To see death and destruction on both sides
Carnage, wanton killing, jealousy, yet love everywhere
To hope beyond hope that life is just an ebbing tide.

To see in the enemy the love of a child
To see the wife, the family, the home
And on both sides all that is domiciled.
To recognise the other humanity is to dig your tomb.

Why do we feel so much hate
What have we been trained for if not for peace.
Everything is done not for me but for the sake of state
Where power is everything a stately cheat.

So join with me, with the view of the dust in the Western sky
Let us join together across the divide
To lay down our weapons and let our souls fly
Until they come once again, the orders above for which we die.

Do not despair my friend
There is a greater good
From the other side of life I'll send
All that is now, not yet understood.

So hold onto the hope of life and love
Never give up the struggle against hate
But remember whatever you feel of hate and love
The answer begins right here in your heart.

Armistice

If only I had decided to remember
Then, then now I have decided to re-examine,
That which has so affected me, so I could return.
I could if I so wished now revisit
The places, the people, to go over and ensure history is recovered.
Purely in my mind I have the power to re-engage
What has long since gone, to find old embers and re-ignite
The situations, the conflict, the passion, maybe the old reprobate.
For people are the cause, deliberately or otherwise, relinquishing
Authority, humanity, love, discipline, perhaps responsibility.

If we can look observe, not to see it all as remedial
And not to be negative, no steps back should be retrograde.
Rather to begin to comprehend this revolution
Of the worlds previous order, was it all a rehearsal?
For now, this is the life, that should be, do we resemble
A divine image of what is meant to be or have we got it wrong;
irrevocably.
For looking back we are tempted to see the hurt personified and
the evil renegade
Then the temptations from the base emotions to seek revenge
Although the nicer of us, perhaps the middle class term it
retribution.
History has taught us the most damning of intellectual pursuits is
reparation.

A politicians revenge, this art of financial recompense,
As if love, so forcibly removed
Can ever be bought; instead we cause the underlying tensions
only to re-evolve.

Cont.

If we truly believed in a better world then we would re-evaluate,
Seek peace, justice and with our enemy find reconciliation.
Blame, defence, blame, and then retaliation
Doesn't actually lead to a world which has been redefined
On God given principles which each and every day in our hearts
he recreates.
To find a world that in our hearts, in our communities and beyond
that rejuvenates

The love of God in each of us, takes away any notion of seeking
retorsion,
Rather it can only be by seeking God's gift of redemption;
Forgiveness is the greatest gift from God to us which we then
replicate
To each other, else the gift from our redeemer
Becomes so pointless. We need to reconcile
With a purity of heart where we are only interested in
resuscitating
A shared world, the breath of peace and reconciliation,
Then everything we experience is worth remembering.

Quiet Transmission

Now tell me what you see
As we sit here, you and me.
Whiling the days one by,
Wishing they'd return, with a sigh.
For we've both gone on in different ways
You to God and me to stay.
And now with memories left
The quiet transmission of love that was left unsaid.

The memories we shared are so true
Of everything we wish for, planned to do.
This is what I truly miss,
What we shared, our wedded bliss.
I would call the love we shared
A love as rich as sunlit air.
For the times we shared were more than plans
They were stolen moments holding hands.

The picture of you in your chair
Me in the kitchen without a care.
Now those days have gone by
The world rests heavy, oh I wish to fly.
Like a bird to lands away and anew
To where you are, just to be with you.
The memories bring tears again
My prayers sometimes, little more than; "Amen".

You see my life has changed
Since you've been gone. To exchange
Anything for you to have just one moment,
Instead of pretending satisfaction at others condolence.
My past is all I've got when you'd once been
My only future. Now only the thoughts of what have been
So give me a little hug as you used to do,
I'll be content sending my love from me to you.

First World Question

When things go wrong, And life gets tough
We sing the same song,, "We've got it rough!"

When we look around At all we can see;
we stand up proud And cry, "Why me?"

Has God picked you, To suffer with pain
Whether it be the flu, Or whatever, you own the blame.

But rather than ask, "Why me, why me?"
Take a look at the past, Take a look, really see.

There's nothing that answers, Why you and not them.
Life is full of chances, Take or ignore them.

But each time you sit, And look at life good and bad
Don't try and fit, Your religion into your hand.

Open it out, open your eyes, And reflect clearly to see
The real question to sigh Is, "Why not me?"

The End

The end is nigh
Or so they say
But I believe will come again another day.

The road is wide
Or so it seems
I believe you can change reality with a dream.

The clock is ticking
Moving faster
But never make time your ultimate master.

The life you've lived
It is plain to see
Is simply to love; simply to be.

The work is done
It is time to sleep
Tomorrow will bring yet more to keep.

FRED IS A
Black Cat
WHO LIVES
NEAR ME

*A simple way to
Reflect Theologically*

Written by Chris McQuillen-Wright
With illustrations by Tim McQuillen-Wright

Introduction

"Fred is a Black Cat Who Lives Near Me" is primarily a basis for theological reflection. Of course it is a story, not a particularly enthralling story as stories go, but a very positive and simple way to begin to theologically reflect.

Theological reflection is something we all do. Who is God? Does God love me like I love my cat? Does God love me? How do I know? How does God view creation? How does my life answer these questions? Why did I think of them in the first place?

"Fred is a Black Cat Who Lives Near Me" is a simple story to help us all easily begin to reflect on our experiences of life and God. No explanations are necessary. Helpful hints would give bias to the reader and hinder the discovery that reflection is really easy.

If you are stuck and find grappling with this is difficult, think to yourself in each situation,

"Am I Fred?", "When am I Fred", "How does this part of the story reflect my understanding of God, or perhaps provoke a side of God I hadn't considered before?"

There are no right answers. There are, therefore, no wrong answers. Whatever thoughts this story provokes in you, are good constructive thoughts.

The easiest way to theologically reflect is to think through the ideas provoked in you, and then discuss them with a friend who has also read the story. In many ways you will agree, in many ways you won't. Either way you are encouraging your spiritual growth. Read it, think about it, play ideas around it, theologically reflect with it. It may provide the catalyst to deeper reflections about God and us, or is it us and God?

Fred is a black cat who lives near me; he really lives with me, but he does not see it that way. Rather, we share an area by mutual agreement. Well, mutual agreement is overstating the issue a bit. He realises he has no choice, after all I was here first and I chose him to live with me. He maintains the freedom to leave at any time, and therefore for some quirky reason he believes that he actually had the freedom to come in the first place. Anyway, Fred and I share this territory, which I would call the house and the garden.

When Fred first arrived he was very unsure of himself; I can still remember him tentatively exploring about, and doing things and eating things he should not. It took a long time for him to learn. He is still learning, because only yesterday he ate something he should not have done and it had a really peculiar effect. He will not eat it again.

Fred is a very resourceful cat. Very soon he knew the house well and so he decided to break out into the garden. I am unsure of whether he realised that I had left the door open for him or not, but he took his first steps out into the garden. He smelt the flowers and he smelt the weeds. Now, I know weeds do not smell, but Fred had not seen one before so he did not know.

My garden is very untidy. I do not have a lawnmower and so for Fred it is like a jungle. It is not very big either, but I keep three chickens in it, and Fred soon learnt that he could not boss chickens about and all of them now get along fine.

Fred has now grown up into a big black cat. Though he is big, he is not fat. He is a very fit, muscled cat, because he looks after himself. He exercises each day, he eats well and takes plenty of rest. He also has lots of energy and runs around protecting the house and garden. He says he defends it for me; but I don't need it defending. For my house and garden are open to all. You don't have to buy a ticket. I have spoken to Fred about it, saying that I do not need a guard keeping other creatures out, for everyone is

welcome. Fred though of course doesn't see it this way.
To him, the house and garden are his territory to protect
against intruders. I don't understand why, but Fred
does.

It is interesting that these intruders to Fred are
other cats. Dogs, birds, flies and bees are allowed in. Or
is it that Fred cannot
prevent them
coming in and
so has to
rationalise
his beliefs?
Dogs
and birds
are allowed
because,
well, because
of some
intensely intelligent
and theological
reason that no one can
understand. Cats are not allowed in the
garden.

I don't really see why, they can hardly make a mess.
The garden is a total mess with weeds everywhere so
having other cats in would probably make it a better
place. At least the grass would be trampled down a bit

more. Anyway, you would have thought that Fred would like to have some friends round to play. But no!

I have known that Fred has been like this for some while. It was today though that I suddenly realised just how vehemently he protects the garden. This is what happened.

Fred has been poorly with a cold, with lots of sniffs and sneezes. He is a lot better now, but he is still recovering, so, of course, I haven't let him out into the garden in this cold weather we have been having. Yesterday, I was sitting on the settee, reading a book on how to manage your relationships within the workplace and was absorbed in the book. I guess I was very relaxed, and certainly was not fidgeting. I knew that Fred was in the room looking out of the window. I thought he was just day-dreaming. He forgot that I was in the room. Suddenly there came an awful cat-cackle, the kind they make when they are hunting, and Fred was hard against the window with his nose squashed and little clouds of condensation forming on the glass.

I keep ornaments on the window sill, so when Fred leapt off he took a few of them with him. As he hurried towards the patio door, I had half an inclination to open it for him. Instead, I sat there and watched almost paralysed at the spectacle that was enfolding before my eyes. Fred hurtled round the room and round the house knocking all sorts of things over as he darted from one window to another. And why?

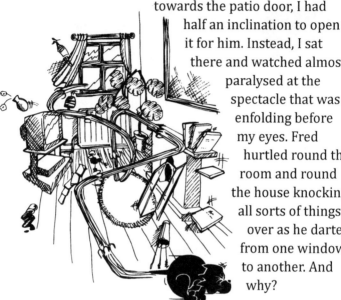

There was another cat, a white tortoise shell cat in the garden - in his garden! Fred was incredulous and implored me to let him out so that he could defend our garden against this intruder.

"Isn't it great", I said. "Another cat coming to be with us."

Fred implored, until it slipped out that he thought the garden was his garden, "After all", he said, "I am the one that walks in it, sleeps in it and hunts in it, sometimes."

I picked Fred up and cradled him in my arms as I had since he was a kitten. I did not want to chastise him, he did not understand that the world was a much wider place than he imagined. Fred leapt out of my arms; and sprung to the window. He meowed and cried. I picked him up again,

"Do not distress yourself," I said. "It doesn't matter," I said, tickling him under the chin.

Instead of relaxing, Fred arched his back and using all his strength he levered himself out, Or at least tried to.

For I am bigger, and I am stronger, and there is nothing he can do without me knowing. In fact his thoughts are so visible in his body movements and facial expressions, sometimes I know what he is thinking and feeling at the same time he does.

"Whoops." Fred has leapt up onto my desk as I write. "Would you say that I can read you like a book Fred? You know the times when you pretend that you really aren't paying attention to me when I am unwrapping fresh fish? You look so self-controlled, giving the impression that you don't care that I have fresh mackerel. You want me to leave the room believing that you won't pounce on it and eat it."

Fred replies, "But you love only me, no one else?!"

"You are special, Fred, there is no one like you."

"So you don't love then other cats then?"

"I have so much love, Fred, I cannot help but love everyone, and I wish you would too. It would make your life so much easier if you didn't get upset about things that are not important. You could hurt yourself running around the house trying to defend the garden, and what for? The garden is for everyone. Please try and welcome them in. My love is all you need.

THE END